THE HIGH PAID
MUSICIAN MYTH

How Smart Musicians Start a Business
to Create Passive Income Before
The High Paid Gigs Come to an End

John O.Reilly

Copyright © 2015 Maverick Musician, LLC.

All Rights Reserved. No part of this publication may be reproduced or transmitted in any form or by any means, mechanical or electronic, including photocopying and recording, or by any information storage and retrieval system, without permission in writing from the author or publisher (except by a reviewer, who may quote brief passages and/or show brief video clips in a review).

Disclaimer: The Publisher and the Author make no representation or warranties with respect to the accuracy or completeness of the contents of this work and specifically disclaim all warranties of fitness for a particular purpose. No warranty may be created or extended by sales or promotional materials. The advice and strategies contained herein may not be suitable for every situation. This work is sold with the understanding that the Publisher is not engaged in rendering legal, accounting or other professional services. If professional assistance is required, the services of a competent professional person should be sought. Neither the Publisher nor the Author shall be liable for damages arising therefrom. The fact that an organization or website is referred to in this work as citation and/or potential source of further information does not mean that the Author or the Publisher endorses the information, the organization or website may provide or recommendations it may make. Further, readers should be aware that internet websites listed in this work may have changed or disappeared between when this work was written and when it is read.

Interior and Cover Design by:

Rory Carruthers

www.RoryCarruthers.com

For more information about John O.Reilly or to book him for your next event or media interview please visit: www.JohnOReillyLive.com

In Memory of

Martin Dennis Reilly

1941-2014

Simply the Best Brother

one could ever hope to have…

The Why

There is a certain group of people whose ranks are growing, who, when they find a problem, feel compelled to discover a way to solve that problem comprehensively for everyone, forever. Not just it a little bit, not just a few minor points of it, but to attack the full problem head on and solve it. This group is a breed apart, the forward thinkers who are all in alignment with what many are calling...

The Age of Voice.

Table of Contents

Introduction 1
Chapter 1   The Talk 5
Chapter 2   Broken Arrow 9
Chapter 3   Value of You 13
Chapter 4   You Are Not a Business, Yet 23
Chapter 5   Position of Power 29
Chapter 6   Do as They Do, Not as They Teach 33
Chapter 7   Expert Business Idea Wanted 37
Chapter 8   Carpe per Diem 41
Chapter 9   The Opportunity We've Been Given 45
Chapter 10   It's the List, Chucklehead 51
Chapter 11   Age of Voice 57
Chapter 12   Those We Leave Behind 61
Chapter 13   Get Busy Living or Get Busy Dying 65
Epilogue 69
Acknowledgements 71
Resources 73
About the Author 75

Introduction

At 62 years of age, realizing that I am more than halfway through my time here on this planet, the sudden passing of my brother really put my entire life into perspective. Couple that with the passing of four other people in 2014 that I had worked with, one passing on my birthday at 63, the other at just 58 this past winter, and two dear friends in September and October, both in their 50s.

It's been a real kick in the ass, and trust me, I've had my share during the once glorious days of the music business. The decline of the music business and the trickle-down effect it's having on musicians everywhere is what this book is partially about. It is also about what you need to be doing right now to take responsibility for yourself and provide for your loved ones.

A forewarning here. There's a lot of colorful language on these pages, so if you're easily offended, too bad, it's the way I speak. I make no apologies for it. Ready?

The music business is fucked. That's not an opinion, it's a stone cold fact that even I have to admit. Although I wrote about the trickle-down effect it's having on musicians everywhere at every level, my primary focus is on the high paid hired gun because I am one, and I can speak with authority on the subject. I won't be trotting out my artist affiliations here or how many platinum records I've recorded and toured on; you can just Google my name or find me on Facebook for that.

This is not a book on how to become a high paid hired gun. Except for a rare occasion, the days of mentoring musicians to do just that are behind me. My main business focus is on my current music gig and consulting on live events, as well as advising artists on how to position themselves, grow a mailing list, and create a real business. Let me clarify this here and now. Just because you have a Corporation or LLC, and you are a sole musician funneling your income into that business account, you do not have a true business. Don't believe me? Stop working and see what happens. Being a musician who is dependent upon playing music as your sole means of income is a broken business model. We'll dive deep into that throughout this book.

I won't be sugarcoating anything in this book either; it's just not my style and might even be considered blasphemous by some of my peers, shit maybe all of them. I'm a 62-year-old rock drummer about to pull back the curtain and reveal the elephant in the room. Sadly, many won't want to hear it, but that's okay, there's still plenty of cardboard they can stuff in the bottom of their boots. One of the cool things about getting older, yes believe it or not there are cool things to getting older, is having to stand less on ceremony than ever. Sometimes, it's just fun to say shit that shocks people. I have a feeling this will get worse as I get older.

I was recently at an informal gathering of friends when I was asked by some snot nose whom I'd never met before what I did for a living. Usually in this case, I would tell them I'm a drug dealer and it would shut them up, but instead I told him I'm a professional musician, at which he sort of scoffed. Sensing the challenge, I asked him what he did for a living, to which he cheerily replied, "I work on Wall Street." I then told him I could learn his job in 90 days or less, but it would take him a fucking lifetime to learn mine. God, I love getting older. But I digress.

Most people, especially musicians, usually riff through a handful of pages from a book at first; however, if you're smart, you'll read the entire thing. The chapters won't be long and drawn out since, these days, time is limited for everyone, so I'll respect yours. I'll also be presenting this book in a live presentation format for those of you who like something a little more immersive and hands on. It will be straightforward, honest, no punches pulled with, of course, lots of drums and a more than a little foul mouthed Irishness. :-)

Text **"maverick"** to **58885** for upcoming live event information.

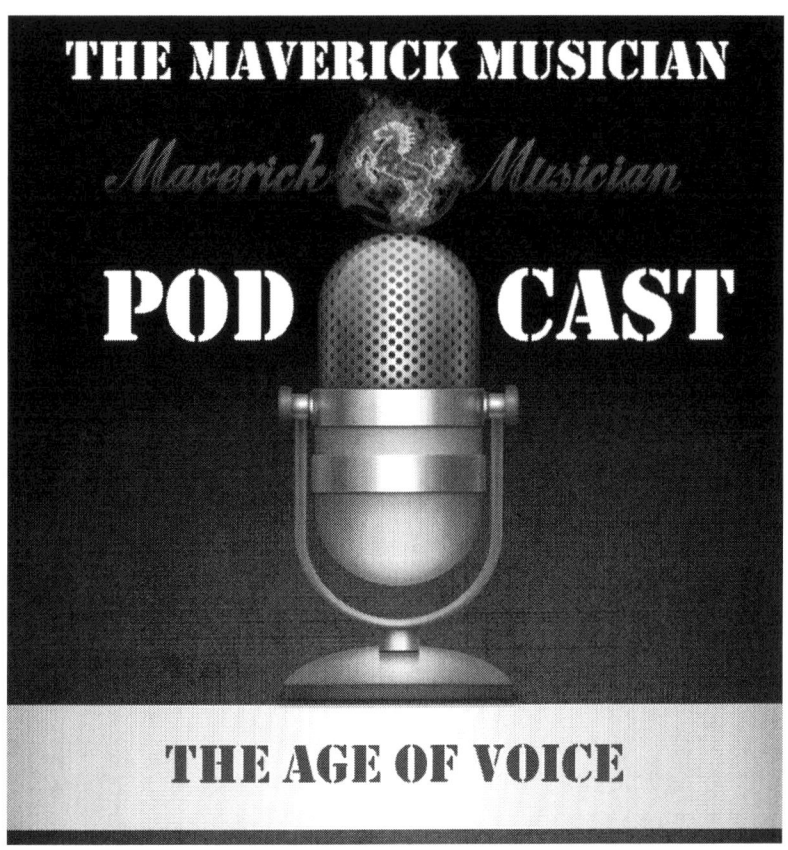
Maverick Musician Podcast

Chapter 1

The Talk

"You have to participate relentlessly in the manifestation of your own blessings."
- Elizabeth Gilbert

In 1970, when I was 18, my big sister's husband knew I was an aspiring musician. He was a fireman, and he tried to convince me to take the civil service test for the FDNY or NYPD as a backup plan in case this music thing didn't work out. He let me know he could arrange things to help with the test. I'm pretty sure my sister put him up to it, not that he didn't like me, but my hair was down to my ass at that time and he referred to guys like me as "Marys." As you may have guessed, I didn't take him up on this offer, but thanked him for his concern. I was certain I would be successful. Although I didn't listen at the time, I know his big heart was in the right place. Sadly, ten years later, he died rescuing his partner while repelling down the side of a burning tenement building, falling seven stories. He is our family's, and my own, personal hero. (God bless you Larry Fitzpatrick, we'll meet again, my friend, but not yet. My brother, Dennis, will keep you busy for now.)

I could probably take it to the bank that if you're reading this book, you've had someone close to you, someone who loves you, give you that same talk. It's universal, a career in the entertainment industry is one of the most challenging, and at the same time heartbreaking, ones you'll ever experience. Speaking for myself, I wouldn't change a thing that I've done to get to where I am now. However, these heartfelt talks are all based on if you fail in the music business.

The question you really have to ask yourself, and the main premise of this book, is what if you are successful in the music business? What does that mean for you? Financial stability? Not likely! Famous? I tend to like this Billy Bob Thornton quote that my business partner Anthony "Tiny" Biuso shared with me:

Essentially, I starved to death most of my life and when I came to California, I beat my brain out for a decade before I could make a decent living. Now there are people who skateboard into a pile of cantaloupes and become famous.

Listen, we all seek fortune and fame at some point in this business. If you're going to really pursue a career in the music industry, shoot for the top, don't fall into the trap of, "I just want to make a living at this, and I'll be happy." I've never met a happy club date musician (they call them casuals in California). Some usually wind up being disgruntled high school music teachers. At least they are teaching and playing music, not digging a ditch at 4:00 A.M. Reach for the top, but don't assume you are going to live a life of luxury as a hired gun.

Lies, lies, lies. Look, no one in the professional teaching world is going to intentionally lie to you. Unfortunately, they just perpetuate the same things they were taught by their teachers, and some of that information will be questionable. The truth is that if you're an intermediate player trying to break into the big time arena/stadium tours/endorsement deals/clinic tours, the odds are incredibly against you. Don't want to pee in your Cheerios, but I warned you; I will not sugarcoat anything in this book.

Don't let that stop you from going for it though because it's a great life. You get to see things, do things, experience things that people who aren't in your position will never experience in their lifetime. It will come with extraordinary sacrifice, which many will not be willing to pay. I won't go down the laundry list here, but I haven't had a Thanksgiving or Christmas at home in well over a decade, and it's especially tough because my dear wife of 14 years has primary progressive multiple sclerosis and requires 24/7 care at our home while I'm traveling during the holidays.

When home, I'm her primary caregiver. We were a blind date in 1997; just a little over a year later, she was officially diagnosed with multiple sclerosis. In October of 2000, we were married, knowing full well what lay ahead for both of us. She is my love, my inspiration, the deep soul connection that you hear stories of and always hope of finding. No sob story here, the pity train doesn't stop at our home. A career of sacrifice; it's yours to choose, you just have to be more than willing to pick up the check for this dream.

Your shortcut to success?

What if that heartfelt talk was changed and focused on creating a business instead of studying for a J.O.B? Back when I was 18, it was virtually impossible. Not only was there no internet, there wasn't even a fucking hint! Now, the barrier of entry is so low that anybody, and I do mean anybody, can start a business, and you do need to start one now, seriously.

The 30,000 foot view. These are the eyes you have to look through to put your career or career aspirations into perspective. Step back and see the big picture, get an overview, and critically scrutinize your situation. Sooner or later, you're going to hit the ceiling for how much you can earn as a high paid hired gun. If your expenses keep pace with your income, when that income stops or the offers for work dwindle down to nothing more than local work, you're screwed. Having other income is essential.

If you are that intermediary guy trying to break into this business looking for that big time gig, why are you only being taught how to be successful at that one thing? The successful musician/arena/stadium/in demand session player clearly has a cap on how much they will ever earn. Think 30,000 foot view.

Chapter 2

Broken Arrow

"In the land of the blind, the one-eyed man is king."
- Desiderius Erasmus

As you already know, the music business will never be the same. The effect these changes will have on the high paid hired gun is inevitable. No, this isn't a long rant on file sharing and illegal downloads because it won't be of service to you and your future in any business you start. You already feel something's coming; it just hasn't raised its ugly fucking head yet. The time to prepare for it is now; the sooner the better, my friend. I ain't kidding.

If you're reading this and have already started a business, either outside of the music industry or related to it, congratulations, you're one of the few, the smart, and forward thinkers who have looked into the void and not seen their reflection. With tour production becoming more expensive every year and the price of diesel through the roof, putting on a large scale tour is just not within the reach of many an artist any longer.

It's not that change is coming, it's already here. It took some time with the free downloading, file sharing Napster thing to virtually dismantle the old major-label business model and put everything and everyone on their rear. In a recent Esquire magazine interview, Gene Simmons was quoted as saying, "Rock 'n roll is finally dead." He was saying that no one is paying for music, and songwriters are getting hit hard. It's impossible to make a living in the music business today. Although the music industry is struggling, I think he jumped the gun on this one.

While Napster and other freeloading, downloading minions slowly dismantled the old music business model, Apple and U2 dropped an atomic bomb, changing everything literally overnight. Now, I'm not privy to the details of their deal (supposedly around $100 million); however, I am impressed with the bombastic results.

Think about it, a company as big as Apple and a band as popular as U2 didn't become successful by taking shots in the dark in the latter years of their success. While the freeloaders inched along and had no idea what they set in motion or the end result, Apple and U2 took one giant step which had an outcome that was easy to predict. Marketplace polarization. It's exactly where they wanted to be, in the headlines of every publication and social media outlet on the planet for days. Did they piss off their true diehard fans? I doubt it. When it showed up on my wife's iPhone, she wanted to send Bono a thank you email. At the end of the day, do you really care if U2 pissed off people who weren't their fans anyway? Yeah, me neither.

It would be foolish to think that other high level artists at this very moment aren't having their own high-powered attorneys trying to hammer out a deal with Apple similar to the one they have with U2. It's a new business paradigm that isn't going away anytime soon. Here's the thing, if an artist can get paid up front for their music to be given away using a carefully structured licensing agreement, how long can ASCAP or BMI last? You tell me. Will they go out of business? I doubt it, but I truly suspect that they'll have to downsize as the majors have.

So, think about this one and try it on for size. If you were a multi-platinum artist who got paid up front to give your music away, would you want to tour? One more question for you. How much do you think U2 spent on recording that giveaway? $500,000, maybe $1 million? Whatever it was, they certainly got a great return on investment and probably something else up their sleeve. Unfortunately, their plans probably don't include many hired guns.

Chapter 3

Value of You

"It may be lonely at the top, but it's so fucking crowded at the bottom."
- Lotus Weinstock

We've all had it, and some of us still dream about it; you know what I'm talking about. It's that ever present thought in our head that sounds something like, "If I could only make $___ a year playing music, I'd be set." Welcome to the magic number, my friend. So, what does it take for you to feel like you're set? Notice I said feel like you're set.

If you are an intermediate player, you no doubt wonder how much somebody who's playing in the so-called big time actually earns per week, right? It really depends on your perception as to who a high paid hired gun actually is and at what level they're performing at (arenas/stadiums or theaters/clubs). The low-end is usually about $1,000 a week, up to $10,000 a week, with the high-end usually being for musical directors; this excludes principal band members. You've seen these bands on television, usually three or four core members upfront and the nameless, faceless dudes hanging out in the back filling out the sound of the band, hoping for some camera time on national television.

Tip - Eye-catching look = camera time.

Okay, let's get to this magic number. It's funny that no matter how many times I ask this question, the answer tends to remain the same from every musician. What's the ideal amount of money you need to make per month touring to be happy?

Answer, $10,000 per month = Happy!

10,000 bucks per month or $2,500 a week is very doable if you can live in that neighborhood. The question is, can you? Or should I ask, do you know how? However, the real question is, how long can you sustain it? With the average tour lasting anywhere between three to six months, with some lasting as long as nine months, the odds of repeating that same touring schedule year after year are slim at best. Not that it can't be done, it's just that it is not in your favor. I told you upfront that I'm not sugarcoating anything, but what the hell do I know?

If you're a single guy earning that kind of dinero and dating, you'll piss away more than you ever thought you would on having fun. You busted your ass to get there, so it's time for a little showing off. It's human nature, just don't be an idiot.

If you're really serious about doing this kind of work, you need to sit down with pencil and paper to figure your number out. I know this seems like a real pain in the ass, but the act of physically writing out this stuff makes it real in your mind and helps you stick to your intentions. Otherwise, it becomes just a bunch of psycho babble in your brain. Everything you do from now on has to be an aim, not just a goal. A goal without an aim is bullshit.

Take a hard look at your expenses, and be brutally honest with yourself. Ask what you need to live really well while playing music for a living. You might not need 10,000 bucks a month, but I'm sure you wouldn't turn it down if it was presented to you for a salary on a world tour. So, how do you get there, how do you get that pie in the sky gig that will pay you what you think you're worth? Like any business tactic, it all starts with a plan. And all plans start at the beginning.

Question - How do you eat an elephant? Answer - One bite at a time!

What are you getting paid locally right now per gig? How many gigs a week are you doing? Are you doing any recordings as a paid session player? Are you doing any paid rehearsals/industry showcases? Other than being a sub on Broadway or doing union jobs in general, all of the above gig pay is negotiable.

Just by increasing what you get paid per gig by 20 bucks will quickly add up, especially if you are doing a decent amount of work in your local area. With this simple act, you've increased your profitability without adding to your workload.

Look, if you don't ask for more money, you won't get it. It's that simple. In my entire career, I've only had one artist give me a pay increase without ever asking for it. It usually never happens in the world of a high paid hired gun. Now, with this newfound increase in income, I want you to do one thing and one thing only with it. Invest in yourself, and nothing else, with four areas of investment.

Appearance, Clothing, Equipment, & Attitude Adjustment.*

*This is free, but the wrong one will cost you.

Now, this might seem really whacked, but bear with me on this. Originally, this was brought to my attention by one of the world's most renowned marketing consultants, Frank Kern. I've twisted it just a little bit to adapt for our purpose here. Any commodity, no matter what it is, has two values; like it or not, music and the people who perform it for a living are a commodity, including myself. We're all regarded as having **practical value** and **intrinsic value**. Even if the people who hire us are clueless to it. So, let's look at this value equation scene.

Practical Value + Intrinsic Value = Total Perceived Value.

Practical value is the thing that you do; you play or sing as well as or better than any other high paid hired gun out there. All things being equal.

Intrinsic value is the unseen perceived value that's created mostly by positioning and promotion. If you add them together, that gives you the total perceived value. Now, let me tell you something that you probably have never heard before...**The money is in your intrinsic value to the gig. It's not in the practical value.**

Value of You

We'll use cars as an example because if you're anything like me, you love a great whip. Let's compare these two rides: a $300,000 Rolls and a $100,000 Beemer. **A $300,000 Rolls-Royce:** nicely done up, very dependable, looks really cool, and a killer ride. **A $100,000 BMW:** nicely done up, again very dependable, looks really cool, and a killer ride as well.

The question we really need to ask is why does the Rolls-Royce cost 300% more, give or take, than the BMW? Especially when you consider that BMW owns Rolls-Royce. A Rolls Royce Ghost is built on the same chassis as the BMW 7 series.

The differences are largely cosmetic. A different body shape and their interior trims are different, a small difference of quality of leather. That might be really debatable in some cases, but that's their real main difference. The difference in price between them is about $200,000. If you ask yourself why the Rolls-Royce is 300% more than the price of the BMW, the answer is this: It's in the **intrinsic value**. Yes, there are some practical value differences, but not $200,000 worth!

Here's the thing – **Rolls-Royce is positioned as the best.**

When something is referred to as the best, it's usually referred to as the Rolls-Royce of_____!

That is what you call global positioning.

Now, this is an extreme example of value equation. You're probably wondering how the hell this relates to you. Ask yourself the following questions:

- How are you positioned in your marketplace?
- How are you perceived?

- What is your intrinsic value to anyone who has the authority to pay you what you're worth as a high paid hired gun?

Attitude is everything when looking for this kind of position, and you can't be a poser or suck at what you do, period. You have to deliver the goods with your practical value!

Increasing your intrinsic value will do two things: it'll increase your profitability and keep you in demand.

Not convinced? Okay, granted, you're not an automobile, you're an artist, right? Alright, let's cut to the chase and get right to art and artists. Can a piece of art have as much intrinsic value as a Rolls Royce? Eben Pagan, who is recognized for his great strategies and techniques for business, marketing, and wealth creation, hipped me to these guys.

Ever hear of Damien Hirst?[1]

---
[1] <http://artweek.la/upload/2654/damien-hirst-spot-paintings.jpg>

Value of You

As of this writing, he is the most successful artist who has ever lived. Net worth somewhere in the $300 millions. Above is one of his spot paintings, a white canvas with different colored spots precisely placed on it. Any guess what one of these goes for? Try about one million bucks. The highest price paid was three and a half million. Here's what's really crazy, there are over 1,300 of them![2]

Still not convinced? Ever heard of Jeff Koons?

He created this:

Balloon Dog (Orange) sold for 55 million dollars. There are 5 of them on the planet, all sold. Do I really need to bring up Andy Warhol? Probably not. Look, these guys get trash talked all the time, "It's not art." Blah, blah, blah, whatever. I couldn't give a rat's ass as far as that's concerned. The point is they're selling, and what really interests me is a comment from a Hirst Spot collector who recently addressed the "It's not art" crowd:

---

[2] "Damien Hirst's Spot Paintings: The Field Guide - The New ..." 2013. 29 Aug. 2015 <http://www.nytimes.com/2013/06/12/arts/design/damien-hirsts-spot-paintings-the-field-guide.html>

No one gets it. Their art is marketing, they've actually elevated their marketing and made it into art, and that's why we love them so much and pay so much for their pieces.

The real kick in the ass is that almost all of these pieces were made by their assistants…Their ASSISTANTS.

These days, like Eben, I'm spending a significant amount of time studying just how the hell these guys have done this, and I'm finding a way to apply it to my own, and my clients', marketing. The reason I included the above in this chapter is to give you hope. To show you the absurd end of intrinsic value while I lay out the reasons why you need to start your own business outside of music, or parallel to it, as you try to break into the world of the high paid musician hired gun.

How do I start to build my intrinsic value if I'm just a local player trying to bust into the hired gun world?

The answer is that you build it through positioning. How would you describe yourself? Are you a **generalist** who does a little bit of every style, whether you play the drums, bass, keyboards, guitar? Maybe your playing is all over the map. Listen, I'm not telling you to forget about studying other styles of music. Any high paid hired gun worth their salt has a deep history in other styles of playing. My first musical love was jazz and big band music; it's what my mother listened to when growing up. However, in 1992, I specialized.

Are you a **specialist?** What style is your prime passion? What are you known for? Is it rock, jazz, r&b, punk? What is it? Being a general player won't serve your best interest here in the realm of the high paid hired gun. The reason is if you don't take a position as to what kind of player you are, someone else will, and you'll probably fucking hate it to no end. However, be honest with yourself, and don't try to be something you're not, something for every situation. Unless the gig you're after requires playing in multiple styles. Then go for it with everything you've got, and nail that son of a bitch.

Specialize. This is when you begin to accumulate intrinsic value as "that player." Always remember this. When the people who are hiring to fill a slot on a tour and are searching for that "high paid hired gun," they're not looking for "a general player," they're looking for "that player." BECOME that player.

Celebrity Authority has the highest amount of intrinsic value there is on the planet. Respect is received without demand and they always appear busy working because they are!

Now, keep in mind that when I use the word celebrity, I'm not talking about it as in the movie star status. However, if Steve Vai was to walk into a room full of guitar players, he is hands down a celebrity in that room. Also, do you think he might be an authority at what he does? Damn Skippy!

There you have it, the **Celebrity Authority.** A distinction he's had for many years, and deservedly so. Is the general public aware of his celebrity authority? Not a clue. It doesn't matter because, as high paid hired guns, we live and work in a microcosm. It only appears that we live and work in the larger world because of movies, television, and social media.

That microcosm illusion that we all live and work in is quickly becoming a diminishing piece of real estate with the flood of more players coming into the marketplace daily. Make no mistake about this. Now is the time to start a business outside of the music industry.

Chapter 4

You Are Not a Business, Yet

*"Go where you are celebrated,
not merely tolerated."*
- Paul F. Davis

Take those above words to heart, and live by them. If it's just you playing music for a living for the long haul, you're hosed! Time for a new bowl of Cheerios, buddy. Hopefully, somewhere in this chapter, I'll be able to convey the reasons why I made that statement. So, let's get on with it and take that 30,000 foot view once again.

Imagine you owned a brick and mortar storefront selling whatever it is you would sell, and you were the only one there, no salespeople, stock people, no one to help you. Now, if you got sick, hurt, injured for just one week, how do you think it would affect your bottom line? It wouldn't be good, that's for sure. What if it was longer than one week? Could you survive one month? Two? A pretty scary thought, right?

Being a high paid hired gun and having a Corporation/LLC puts you in that same position as that brick and mortar store owner working by himself. Very vulnerable to that same scenario of becoming sick or permanently disabled and unable to earn a living. A nightmare that has come true for many of us. I wouldn't wish it on anyone at any time, and I've felt horrible for the guys that I personally know who have had this happen to them. It's like getting punched in the stomach.

This is why a single source of income is the kiss of death for any musician. I really hope to change this notion of waiting until you're successful in music to create other income streams because the inclination here is a mindset limited to an unrealistic timeframe. The sooner you start to create something, the better off you're going to be.

Start a business. I don't care what it is, just do it. Someone, somewhere in the world, will thank you for creating it. Remember that heartfelt talk with my brother-in-law that I referenced in the beginning of this book? Well, this is mine to you right here on this page for better or worse, gruff as it is, take it or leave it. But, I hope you take it.

Now, I know that if you consider yourself a "true artist" a "musician's musician," you're gonna find this entrepreneurial thing beneath you, and that's okay, really. I've been there, but I realized that with a little business savvy, I could make a living for myself beyond what I make as a hired gun. I know I'll be okay when the music gigs stop coming my way.

You might be excited about starting a business, but don't know what to do next. A lot of people get stuck on what to create.

You have something to share with the world. Think beyond the music. One big trend these days seems to be hot sauce. I know several guys who are doing really well with this; don't know anything about it myself, except I like it on my eggs and just about everything else I chew on. I've met guys who scour the country looking for old vintage cars to fix up and sell for a high profit, and there always seems to be some knucklehead somewhere who will pay through the nose for it. Again, not my cup of tea, but maybe it is yours. Shit, I've even met guys who broker deals between people with no inventory, just information. Sometimes the best man is the middleman in any business; is that you?

I would seriously avoid any brick and mortar business, such as rehearsal studios, recording studios, physical locations for music lessons (unless they're in your home), food joints, anything you have to put a sizable chunk of change into because if you fail, you're fucked! You can easily teach anyone music lessons anywhere on the planet via Skype or Google Hangouts. You can even start this while on the road; just start.

Create an online course. There are companies around that will help you put it together for a fee. Write a book. I did, you're reading it now. Don't dare tell me that you can't type because neither can I. I use a piece of software that lets me talk into my computer, and it types onto the screen into a Word document. Ridiculously easy.

Go for the easiest thing you can begin with, let's call this the low hanging fruit, the thing that's within your immediate reach. Stay away from anything that's too aggressive and that you're not comfortable with. Start slow and easy, make a few bucks, and see if it's scalable (if it can it be expanded or not). If you're already a high paid hired gun and you have some celebrity currency, this is the time to cash that shit in.

Listen, I don't want to scare you by writing this, but you know something's coming and it won't be pretty. This is the elephant in the middle of the room! Prepare now or prepare to be hosed in the coming years. Whether you're an aspiring high paid hired gun or if you already are one, the lowest barrier to entry is online because it's the cheapest, and if you fuck up, and you will, you won't lose your shirt. The great thing about starting a business online is that it allows you to fail fast, pick up the pieces, and start over while learning from your mistakes. Since we are musicians, we know all about failure.

Sometimes the learning curve in our music career can take a lifetime. Sadly, some have never recovered from that failure and settled for a life of conformity. It's never too late though... Onward and upward, I say!

One of my businesses, and I have several, creates information products. You might be wondering what the hell that means, so here goes. Solutions to problems that people are having. When you put that solution in front of the right people looking for that solution, and they feel confident in your ability to help them, they will pay you. It's not rocket science.

Here's what I got, here's what it'll do for you, here's what I want you to do next, here's how much it's gonna cost ya!

I also run an online digital drum school that is totally automated with minimal involvement from me, publish a monthly digital magazine on the Apple newsstand that is mostly outsourced, except for the editor's overview, and run two multimedia consulting companies, one for local businesses where I live to broaden their customer acquisition and the other for live event consultations that utilizes auto responders, trigger text messaging, and QR codes all in relation to list building. Additionally, I'm an author with the very book that you're reading. Finally, I also have a business that is boring to the average human being, yet they unknowingly participate with it on a daily basis: Digital sales funnel optimization. Yeah, I know boring. But not to me! Don't forget, I also need to show up for tours, speaking engagements and drum clinics from time to time.

Get my drift? Diversify your business interests.

Once you've become accustomed to thinking outside of the high paid hired gun box and become comfortable with the idea of expanding to other businesses, think of partnerships, building a team of other like-minded players. Remember, if you're going to have different businesses, you should also have different partnerships for them. Having the same group of people across various business entities would be a mistake. I strongly suggest starting each of these different entities by yourself, learning everything you can about them before bringing any form of partnership into the picture.

One problem. One solution.

It doesn't make any difference to me what business you start; just make sure you take to heart the bolded statement above. Every budding entrepreneur or inventor wants to come up with the next day thing. The gazillion dollar idea that every household will want. I'm calling bullshit on that. If you try to create something for everyone, you'll wind up with a lot of something for no one, so don't ever go there.

A perfect example is this book; I've carefully targeted two groups of people. The aspiring high paid hired gun and the hard-core experienced high paid hired gun. Anyone else reading this book, and I thank you in advance, is an unexpected bonus. I'm going to advise you here to start with the written word, the solution to one problem that a large group of people are having and will pay money for that solution. It's the easiest process to do, and the software is available on any computer everywhere.

I'm using Microsoft Word and an older version of Dragon Point & Speak 11.0 because I can't type for shit. Obviously, not being able to type didn't stop me, and it shouldn't stop you. Even if you only have a hint of an idea, start writing. Forget about proper grammar, punctuation, and any such nonsense during this creative process; that's what editors are for. Write and keep writing. One problem, one solution

Chapter 5

Position of Power

"Always come from a position of power."
- Jimmy Ienner

This piece of advice has stuck in my head for a long time, and was imparted to me by my first music mentor and friend for over 40 years. Jimmy Ienner was the producer of the first band I was ever signed to a major label with. I still call him to this day for advice and insight on what's happening with the recording industry from his vantage point, as well as bringing in talent from time to time when I think it's worthy and what we're looking for.

While I gaze from 30,000 feet, he looks out from the stratosphere and sees it all. Now, when I'm referring to a position of power, it's not in any way meant as bullying or taking advantage of someone. It's a subtle force coupled with celebrity authority.

What's your position of power? What can you see that nobody else around you can see? It's here where the position of power has its roots. Many years ago, I entered a drumming event searching for the top drummer in the New York tri-state area. This thing stretched on for what seemed like an eternity, and I went to every elimination that was held.

There was pre-recorded music that everyone had to play along with that had at least eight different breaks in each one. It was pretty obvious to me that a solo was supposed to be inserted into those breaks. Out of 1,800 drummers who entered (500 were in my category alone), not a single one played a solo. They twirled sticks, threw sticks in the air, or just left silence in those breaks by not playing anything at all, some anticipated too early coming back in and dropped a huge sandwich. Needless to say, I won.

I saw something glaringly obvious during those early eliminations and acted upon it without hesitation at the final event. I just couldn't believe that no one had seen what I was able to see. Now trust me, I'm no soothsayer; however, when you know what you're looking at, it is not hard to miss. My stock took an uptick, and I got a drum set to boot. Yay for me!

Many players have no idea what it is that they're looking at on any given day in their daily touring routine. They fall into patterns and walk through their gigs seemingly in a trance. If you're one of those players, snap out of it or be faced with the same outcome day after day, week after week, month after month, year after year until you're dead. Start taking notice of things around you, specifically products. Ask yourself how these products can be improved.

The following exercise might help you get out of the possible drudgery you might be mired down in from day to day. Whenever I see something that piques my interest, I whip out my phone right away and dictate into it before my idea vanishes, then I transfer it by writing it down on paper. The reason I write it down on paper is because it's visceral. It has a sticking factor to it, much more than just the recorded word. When I see those words on paper, I give myself a license to run with them, not daydreaming; a focused train of thought looking for that one solution for one problem. I'm always led away from that original thing that piqued my interest. Sometimes it works, sometimes it doesn't, but that is my process and I'm sticking to it.

I'm not a songwriter, but I do have an interesting songwriting analogy. A while back, I saw Bruce Springsteen on Late Night with Jimmy Fallon. Springsteen was being gushed over about all of the great songs he's written in his career, and in a moment of complete candor he told Fallon, "For every one song that I write, there are at least 25 that are pure crap." Fallon laughed, but was clearly surprised at this unexpected exchange. It's funny how the same process of creation, whether it be songwriting or creating an information product, can be so similar. You'll probably have some crappy ideas, but you'll also have some great ideas that you can share with the world through your business.

Would I trade being a product creator for being a songwriter? Not these days, not a chance. There's way more control in being a product creator, and here's why. It's me, an idea, direct to the marketplace, right into the international hip pocket bank.

The only thing I would change is to have done this sooner.

Chapter 6

Do As They Do, Not As They Teach

"Nothing is more powerful than an idea whose time has come."
- Victor Hugo

Does it seem like everywhere you turn there's an event that wants to teach you to be successful in the music business? The motivational/musical/music business event is becoming popular (for drummers in particular), and I'm glad for it to be so. All of these events, to my knowledge, are top notch in their professionalism and have raised the bar from the typical clinic environment that requires a slide rule.

They're a combination of edutainment, lifestyle and music, not to be confused with the so-called music fantasy camps that usually upwardly mobile hobbyist musicians will pay $5,000 for being coached by a rockstar to have their dream of performing with them fulfilled. Trust me here, I'm not knocking this. If somebody has the ability to fulfill a lost dream and the cash to do it, God bless 'em, boy howdy. Whether you approve it or not, it's a cash cow, and someone's taking it to the bank big-time by creating a business out of it. No judgment here.

Here's the point. Neither of these style events are preparing anyone for the inevitable reality that sooner or later, hopefully much later, the big money gigs will one day be gone. And you'll have that aisle seat to Palookaville…How long can you keep going from one big gig to the next without huge swings both upwards and downwards in your income? Probably not very long. That is, unless you're prepared.

It's my intention to have you see what others around you are not seeing. To make you aware that just learning how to be a successful musician is nowhere near enough to provide you and your loved ones with the safety of an additional business that provides you an extra income, whether you are an employed high paid hired gun or you're trying to be. Like I stated above, many of my peers are presenting these "success in music" events, or music camps as some are called, and I think it's fantastic, with one exception.

Even though they are clearly demonstrating an entrepreneurial spirit by expanding their own positions as a high paid hired gun, teaching the hopeful on how to be a successful musician in the world today, they're not teaching them the very thing that they are doing themselves as entrepreneurs. Why is that? I don't think they're doing it on purpose, I think it's more like not seeing the forest through the trees in front of them.

They're just too close to the subject at hand, not realizing just how important teaching entrepreneurialism is to this hungry, enthusiastic bunch. They're busy teaching the business of music and how to become successful at it, and not teaching the skill of creating a real business and becoming successful at that.

If you are an aspiring high paid hired gun, I'd like you to start paying attention to what your teachers are doing, not just what they are teaching. When I say teachers, I don't just mean in the literal sense that you're paying someone for lessons or to attend an event, which I recommend you do. I'm speaking of all successful musicians because they all have something to teach you, whether you realize it or not.

Research their other business interests, be it putting on live events or being part of a production house; there are countless examples of players who enhanced their careers as musicians by becoming entrepreneurs. Our entire business has been turned upside down. Check it out. There are artist management companies right now who are advising their new artist signings to think about creating their own fragrance or clothing line. This is before they're successful. I shit you not.

The stigma of an artist selling out has seemingly disappeared. I can remember hearing Zeppelin on that Cadillac commercial years ago and thinking to myself, "Hmmm, something's coming..." At the time, I had no idea that our business would become what it is. So, what are you going to do about it? Are you going to continue to just buy the dream? It's a beautiful dream, and I'm living it. But sooner or later, and I truthfully hope it's sooner, you'll realize that there is a cap on what you will be able to earn and a limited time you'll be able to earn it...as just a high paid hired gun.

There will probably be some of my "Musician Musician" friends who are going to call bullshit on this book, whatever. Looking through the eyes and experience of someone in their

30s in this business is a lot different than the eyes and experience of someone in their 60s in this business. I've known too many beaten down musicians who have died alone in cheap hotel rooms or some shitty apartment at some point in their waning careers when it didn't have to be. There's nothing romantic about being homeless and broke; I've been there. Here's the really fucked up part, it was my choice to live like that. To roll the dice. However, that's a different book.

Don't ever be afraid to become **that guy** (not the homeless and broke one); you know who I'm talking about. The tireless self promoter with an idea who goes for it. They're the ones who'll create the change necessary for any forward movement in their business/career, usually dragging a kicking and screaming industry in their wake.

Steve Jobs, Bill Gates, Jeff Bezos, and Jim Koch. They all pushed themselves, and in turn, changed their industries for the benefit of many, becoming multi-millionaires as a result. Can you do the same? Never doubt yourself, it's the killer of all dreams and aspirations because it all starts with a dream. After all, you're a musician. We know all about dreams.

Still stuck on an idea? No worries, in the next chapter I'll share with you you an exercise that was taught to me. Once you do it, you'll be amazed at what might be in that head of yours once you put it onto paper. It's pretty powerful and worth your time.

You'll need a timer. Paper. Pencil. That's it.

Chapter 7

Expert Business Idea Wanted

"The quality of our lives is directly proportional to the quality of questions we ask."
- Tony Robbins

Am I looking for an expert business idea? Always. I hope that by doing this exercise, you'll find an idea for a business to start, or maybe you might have an idea already that you might change after completing this exercise. You might be surprised! Like I wrote above, you'll need some sort of timer, something to write on, and something to write with to get started.

1) Set a timer for 2 minutes.
2) **Write down a skill you would like to master as a possible business idea**, no matter whether you think you can master it or not. (Examples: hypnosis school, cable television

cooking show, teach independent film production, becoming an author, public speaking, music school etc.) If you get stuck, just write, "what's next…" over and over again until something pops into your head; you'll get bored quickly and something will show up.

3) **Once your 2 minutes are up, immediately stop writing.** Take a 1 minute break to clear your head. Get up from the table and walk to another room.

4) **Go back and rate each skill that you wrote from 1 to 5.** One being the least interested in mastering and five being the most interested in mastering. Give yourself **5 seconds** to rate each skill. Remember, it's **5 seconds** on each one, and being quick is a key thing here. I still do this exercise and have gotten pretty fast at it; this is strictly about intuition and not objective thinking.

5) **Go back and circle each skill that you rated as fives, and put them on a separate piece of paper.**

6) **Give yourself 60 seconds** to pick the most enticing skill out of all the skills you gave a value of **five** to. If after 60 seconds you can't choose one, then pick one randomly.

7) **Once you've decided on your skill**, break it down into four major elements. These are the four areas you think are the most important to master. If after 60 seconds you can't decide, then randomly pick between you four areas.

8) **Once you've broken it down into four different areas**, give yourself 60 seconds to choose the first area you like to master. If after 60 seconds you can't decide, then randomly choose between your four areas.

9) **Once you've picked an area**, break it down into three subgroups that you think are the most important for mastering those areas.
10) **For each of these three subgroups**, design a system that will mechanically allow you to gain skill and knowledge in that area with as little conscious thought as possible. The best systems are checklists, reference guides, processes, and step by step exercises.
11) **Once you come up with a system** for each of these subgroups, then go to work until you become comfortable using those systems. Once that is done, go back to the three remaining areas that you broke down.
12) **Pick one of the three remaining elements**, break that down into three remaining subgroups, and repeat the process. Do this until you have mastered all four elements. Then you'll be an expert at a skill that can be used as the foundation for your new business.

If you are new to this kind of process, and you probably are, don't freak out and say, "Screw it, this is bullshit." This is only an exercise to jog what's inside of your noggin. You've been given the greatest gift of all, your consciousness and the ability to think in the future with clear focus and intention. Your gifts are not for nothing, find a way to share your expertise with the world, maybe you should write a book about it.

Business to Create Passive Income Before The High Paid Gigs Come to an End- Reilly, John O.

Chapter 8

Carpe Per Diem

"Carpe Per Diem - Seize the check!"
- Robin Williams

How do you seize that check? In my opinion, the easiest way to do this is by writing a book to position yourself in the marketplace that you've chosen. Nice segue, right?

The most effective way to come up with what your book should be about is to ask the **really important questions** from the very marketplace that you can thrive in. Start by coming up with 15 or 20 counterintuitive questions to get the ball rolling, and begin the process of putting it all together.

Here it is.

1) **Record the answers** to your 15 or 20 important questions. A smart phone works great for this.
2) **Get it transcribed.** There is a website called Fiverr you can use. Or you can buy the software I use called Dragon Point & Speak for about 100 bucks.

3) **Edit it**. Or hire someone if you have to. Don't worry about making it perfect; I sure as hell didn't.
4) **Give it some cool cover art**. Again, you can use Fiverr for that if you want.
5) **Give it away**. Or sell it for $.99. You'll have that option once you publish to Amazon's KDP Kindle platform.

These answers should take you about 10 minutes each. I'm guessing that's roughly 150 minutes or so worth of content. One hour of spoken word equals about 40 pages of written word. In the above example, that's about 100 pages. Also, I'd like you to think of your content in this way, create something that's counterintuitive. In other words, focus on something that is not common knowledge.

You'll find that by giving them something that they would not normally hear about, they will become the best marketers in spreading your word and what you do. The best form of marketing has always been word-of-mouth from the people you've helped and not just you talking about yourself. That gets old really fast, especially on social media like Facebook.

I already know your number one question. If I give my book away or just charge the measly $.99 per copy, how the hell am I going to seize the check? You don't, not with this one at least. Your book is only going to be used as a positioning tool for leveraging possible speaking engagements and interviews and not for any real monetary consideration through its sale. Taking this book's content and repurposing it is what you will do, creating videos, short articles, and podcasts to create a multicast effect across the interwebs. Use the practical value of your book in many ways while you increase your intrinsic value as its author.

When you ask quality questions of importance, you'll get quality answers. It really is that simple. Maybe a few of you have already published a book yourselves with less than great results. There's a definite reason for that, somewhere, somehow you screwed up the process. No worries, in this next chapter, I will show you what I mean. Let's sort this out, shall we?

Chapter 9

The Opportunity We've Been Given

*"You can lead a horse to water,
but you can't make him drink."*
*"I really don't care, because
I can make 'em thirsty."*
- O.Reilly

Cause and effect cannot be escaped. Even though the book publishing industry hasn't gone through the same upheaval that forced the music business to reevaluate its current lack of power, it is going through its own revolution. The cause, in this instance, is the 800 pound gorilla in the room, Amazon. The effect is, you guessed it, anyone can publish their own book. The barrier of entry into this market has vanished.

Did you know that Amazon will allow you to upload just your book cover and take pre-orders? That's right; you're able to test the interest in your subject matter before ever writing a word. Did I mention it costs you nothing out of pocket to do this? You're also allowed to position your price point wherever you want it to be. Want to charge money for it? No problem. Want it to be free and share it with everyone? No problem.

Hopefully, I'm making this so painfully obvious that you won't be able to ignore it. The only thing that's standing in your way is you! There is no such thing as lack of opportunity any longer, no such thing as it takes too long to learn the technology to pull this kind of thing off. I'm calling bullshit on all excuses.

If I can't entice you with the entrepreneurial Kool-Aid, I hope I have made you a little bit thirsty as to question your position in the music industry. At least if you're still reading up to this point. Still here? Good, let's continue. Can you sell physical products on Amazon and be successful? I gave it a shot and bought a high-end course on how to set up an Amazon store. I tried it and didn't like it, too many moving parts, dodgy suppliers, you name it, just wasn't for me. Next.

I prefer simplicity in any business that I create. Automation is what you should strive to attain in your business model. It should be able to run day to day with minimal input from you, and that's why I've chosen information products and consulting as the backbone of my businesses. I know that right now this sounds ridiculously vague to you, and the reason is simple. It's because the concept, the idea, might be brand new. Let's take this book for example, to see if I can clear some things up. This particular book is an information product, make no mistake about it. It's priced relatively cheap, you either paid $.99 for it or possibly it was free. This was intentional, not by chance.

Whether it was free or you paid $.99 for it, you subscribed to my mailing list. I hope that because I've given you something of great value on these pages, you'll stick around on that list. I say **that list** because I have many lists of my own, and clients' lists as well.

I don't have to tell you that customers are the backbone of every business, but more importantly, their contact information is crucial to your success. We'll talk in-depth about this in an upcoming chapter. I just want to point out the difference between a book that's an information product and one that delivers totally different content with a completely different intent. Some other intents are:

1) Traditional storytelling. (No list building intent)
2) How to or Trade books. (No list building intent)

Both of those examples are working off the old model where you write the book and make money on the sales from it. **Publishing**. Does that sound familiar? It should because it's the old record business model! And we know where that went, down the toilet. Look, am I advising you to forget about concentrating on the above examples? Absolutely not! The world needs great storytellers with the pure intention of helping the world, or at least that group of people searching for the comfort their words provide. As far as trade books, they'll continue to do well. However, if I need to figure out how to do something, you can bet your ass I'm going to YouTube for that. There's always some kid somewhere who's figured out how to do something that I don't know how and made a video about it. Especially if it has to do with computers, because I suck at it.

Do you know anyone who doesn't have an Amazon account? Can you count them on 10 fingers? Personally, I can't think of one of my friends who isn't on Amazon. So, this opportunity that we've all been given is truly open ended, an opportunity with little or zero cost to start with no limit on what you can earn through it.

What creative model that you know of can offer this opportunity to you? Songwriting? Don't make me laugh. All things being equal, let's look at what would happen if you were to square off a talented songwriter with a publishing deal and a talented information product creator with a small email list of 1,000 people and let them do what they do.

Songwriter: Write a song from scratch, submit it to their publisher, wait for a response, and maybe make money from it. **Information Product Creator:** Create an information product that solves a real problem and gives value, send it to a targeted segmented portion of their list linked to a PayPal account, wait for a response and make money from it.

The information product creator will eat the songwriter's lunch every day. Direct to market is the fastest way to money. To put it another way, money loves speed, and you won't find any faster way when no one is in the middle, like a publisher or even a manager for that matter.

As we get near the end of this book with the final chapters, I'd like you to step back and take the 30,000 foot view. Retrace your steps to the purchase or acquiring of this book, to follow the marketing that was used. Did you follow a link from Facebook or somewhere else?

You went through a carefully crafted sales funnel that one of my other businesses specializes in. Digital sales funnel optimization. I guarantee you go through one or more of these every day, whether it's Amazon, iTunes, or any web property in retail. An AIDA sales funnel. The acronym is for: awareness, interest, desire, and action, whether it's brick and mortar or digital. Don't just read this book and take it at face value, study how you got here.

Eye opening, isn't it? If you find any of this interesting and would like more information just text: **maverick** to **58885** on your mobile phone, and I'll hook you up. Maybe we can work together in the future!

Chapter 10

It's In the List, Chucklehead

"Welcome to the machine."
- Roger Waters

After struggling online for a few years, I finally broke down and realized I couldn't figure this shit out by myself. I had to hire someone, but whom? We're talking 1998 here, and there was a huge void on the internet about this. In fact, I had just purchased my first computer and clearly had no idea what I was doing. Scams were everywhere, and I bought into a few without having any virus protection, malware protection, zip.

I had purchased a piece of software that scraped email addresses from websites, which in return sent an email promoting my product! Within a very short period of time, I received the blue screen of death and lots of threatening e-mails with the subject line: **FUCK YOU, SPAMMER!!!!!!!!**

I was an idiot.

That's when I hired my first one-on-one mentor. His name is Claude Diamond, and he taught me about sales, lease purchasing, real estate, and success coaching. A brilliant strategist and success coach in his own right, and for whom I'm eternally grateful to still be in contact with to this day.

He had a hard copy newsletter that he sent out every month. It was the first time that I've ever heard of a client list. This is where the rubber meets the road, no list = no business.

I am continually surprised by how many people in the arts and entertainment field just don't get this. How do they think business happens? If you're still having a problem wrapping your head around this, I'd like you to pay attention to the next big movie release that's coming up, whatever one, it doesn't matter. Big movie releases always use a launch formula, one that is very exact and elicits a specific result. Whether it's a horror film, science fiction, romance, you get the point. It's not left to chance, especially when millions of dollars are at stake. You'd be a fool to think otherwise because these movie studios are fighting for their virtual lives.

The flipside is rather than using the above launch scenario, which is very old school, marketing to a specific niche is already here and becoming eerily personal. Have you been noticing different advertisements following you around all over the internet? Some people are placing the blame on big companies like Amazon or iTunes when, in fact, it's not of their making at all. Various companies put tracking pixels on their websites. When you visit a website, a little smidgen called a pixel is attached to you online so that everywhere you go online you will see an advertisement for that company. You can try to disengage from this kind of advertising all you want, but in the end you won't be able to, unless you just want to read a newspaper. There's always the funny papers every Sunday. They can't track your ass there. However, it's going to get even more pervasive.

Soon it will not only be on your computer, but on all smartphones, tablets, and smart televisions on a global scale. Advertising specifically designed for you by using all of the personal information you have given with consent to all the social media sites you've signed up to. It's the biggest list in the world.

Seriously, you need to be building a list of people, prospects, fans, call them whatever you want because this is serious. If you're not serious about your career, than what the hell are you doing? Listen, I'm not asking you to become a douchebag about this, far from it. You don't need to have tracking pixels on your website, but you do need to generate a list to keep track of customers and potential customers.

On a smaller level, this technology is already available to you, if you choose to use it. It's all about business, and the money is in the relationship that you have with your list. I know some artists who are afraid to sell anything to anyone who is on their list because they are worried that they will unsubscribe. If they're not buying anything from you anyway, who cares if they leave? That argument never made any sense, yet I still hear it from time to time.

To build your list, you are going to need what's known as an autoresponder. This is a piece of software that stores email addresses and names, and lets you send out emails either in the form of a broadcast message or sequence event. Just about everyone I know in the music field usually sends out a broadcast message, or email blast, once in awhile to their list. The problem with sending out a broadcast message for most is that they become lazy and forget to do it on a regular basis.

What happens next is that your list grows cold or unresponsive to any offers or news that you might want to share with them. Setting up an automatic sequence that keeps them in the loop is the only way to avoid this because it keeps them engaged with what you're doing. Keep in mind that you are not constantly clobbering them with offers; never do that. These people have raised their hands and said, "I trust you," by giving you their information, don't ever betray that trust. If you owned a store on Main Street and betrayed the trust of a customer, do you think they'll be back? I know I wouldn't.

Speaking of Main Street. At a recent SXSW conference, speaker Gary Vaynerchuk was giving the Keynote address and related this true story.

He and some friends were looking for a place to grab a meal and called ahead to a well-known restaurant that was a little hard to get a table at. The party was told if they could get there within 10 minutes or so, they could have a table. They got there in about 5 minutes, but were told that the table was gone. Of course, they were visibly disappointed. One of them whipped out his cell phone and intensely started to type away while trying to get reservations at another restaurant. The maître d' saw this, presumed that they were now about to get a bad review online, and quickly found them another table.

So, the next time you get screwed out of a table, take out your cell phone with intent. Hey, you never know, it just might work for you if you get screwed out of a table some night.

Social media is powerful, just make sure you are making it work for you, not against you!

You can check out one of my businesses right here: Just text **777** to **58885** or scan the QR code below.

Chapter 11

Age of Voice

"Even one voice can be heard loudly all over the world in this day and age."
- Aung San Suu Kyi

Are you a creator or a consumer? If you're a creator, what will your content be? If you're a consumer, what's holding you back from creating? Those are the real questions. If you're a songwriter/lyricist, you already know all about the creative process and the frustration that comes with it. So, when an organization like The Recording Academy is urging its members to either write or call, and if possible set an appointment with, their local congressman to advocate for their rights as music creators, something is terribly wrong. I don't know about you, but that's a big ass red flag, and waiting for Congress to take action on your behalf is a fucking joke without a punchline. The time to shift, or at least augment what you are doing, is now.

I recently read that in 2014, only 60 digital songs sold 1 million copies compared to 83 the year before. After almost a full year, not one artist's album has hit the 1 million unit mark. **Another big ass red flag?**

Can the music business be saved? If you were to ask me that three years ago, I would've said maybe. I think the tipping point has truly been reached with the next generation already accessing the internet and downloading the latest music for free. With the average 13-year-old having a smartphone or tablet, or both, getting access to the latest free music only requires an email address and the willingness to download. The idea of paying for music to this generation would be like asking them to pay for breathing, unless of course you shut it off. It ain't gonna happen, not in my lifetime, and maybe not even yours, or your children's.

Listen, you can ignore it, rail against it, fight tooth and nail for what once was, or you can adapt and prosper in different ways. Even the savviest musician/entrepreneurs that I know aren't just relying on selling their music; they all have other business interests. These aren't multiplatinum artists that you've heard or read about; they're just working musicians trying to make a buck at what they love, and you can do the same. And should.

We live in a time that I like to call the Age of Voice, an audience for all of us. There has never before been a time in the history of humanity where a simple click would allow someone to receive your message, your help, your solution to any problem anywhere in the world in seconds flat right to their smart phone. Just 10 years ago, this ability didn't even exist. With platforms like Amazon, YouTube, Facebook, and a whole slew of other social media sites allowing you to do this, it's virtually free to you. If you have a little money for advertising, coupled with the right knowledge, your reach and solutions are unlimited when aimed at your chosen market. Did you realize you're carrying a television station in your pocket that can broadcast to the world?

95% of all mobile phone users keep their phone within arm's reach 24 hours a day. 50% of the average global mobile users now use mobile as either their primary or exclusive means to access the internet. 73% of the human race is engaged with social media right now. There are billions of people accessing the web from their mobile device right now.[3]

The really big picture here is delivering and distributing high-quality, engaging content that's gonna have an immediate positive impact on people's lives on a global scale. That's what I, and my companies, stand for.

What we stand against is anything that smacks of bullshit, like push a button and make a million bucks while hanging out in your underwear, or other such nonsense that doesn't exist. Unfortunately, just about everyone falls for that crap when they first enter the online world; it's almost a rite of passage. One I sincerely hope you can avoid if you're at the beginning of this journey into entrepreneur land.

---

[3] "Mike Koenigs - Chief Disruptasaurus, #1 Bestselling Author ..." 15 Sep. 2015 <http://mikekoenigs.com/>

Chapter 12

Those We Leave Behind

"Our death is not an end if we can live on in our children and the younger generation. For they are us, our bodies are only wilted leaves on the tree of life."
- Albert Einstein

You might be under the impression that my strong urge for you to create a business is my one size fits all answer. Believe me, it's not. What I'm about to reveal to you is something you most likely never thought of as being an important step in the life of a professional musician.

Get life insurance. Yes, that's right, life insurance. Be honest here, did you ever think of it? I just don't talk the talk, I walk the walk, so yes, I have it for my family. Here's a question for you. Can you afford $40 a month? That's about $1.33 a day. It's a ridiculously inexpensive way to offer some protection for your loved ones, especially if you have children.

Will you have to jump through some hoops? Of course you will. There will be the obligatory blood test and drug test. Maybe give up the extra money you spend at Starbucks. If nothing else, at least think about this: 40 bucks a month will get you about $150K in benefits for those you leave behind after your unexpected demise. You don't have to start you there, you can start with less. Just start. This is especially the right thing to do if you're unmarried with children because your live in partner can still be the beneficiary of your insurance policy, and at least your children will have something to help them in the future.

Prices are going to vary depending upon your age and your health, because the younger you are and the better health that you're in will determine your monthly premium. If you're in your 30s, now is the time to start this process and get the ball rolling. I know of many in the high paid musician community who are without a solid life insurance policy, or at least one that will pay for their final expenses when the time comes. It will come for each and every one of us sooner or later. That's one guarantee you can absolutely count on.

I've almost died three times in my life, all by near drowning. The last time was truly life-changing. I was at one of the best parties I had ever attended. It was a July 4th weekend pool party at a fellow bandmates house, and it was rocking! I was 28 or 29 at the time, very single and out-of-control. As I remember it, the ratio was three women to every guy. Excellent hunting, and I was acquiring targets left and right. I was surveying the landscape, standing next to the singer in our band, when I fortuitously mentioned to her that I couldn't swim, "If you see me in that pool at any time today, I'll probably die because of it."

She gave me a rather strange look and acknowledged me, then I was off on the hunt having acquired a target. There she was standing right next to my least favorite place in the world, the in ground pool, shallow on one end, deep on the other. I was not happy, and quite frankly, it scared the shit out of me. That didn't stop me in the least.

After about 10 minutes of the usual small talk and laughter, I turned my head to check out what was happening elsewhere only to feel her hand slowly intertwine with mine. That cat's grin smile began to spread across my face. I'm in! "September" by Earth, Wind & Fire was pumping. What happened next changed my life.

Unbeknownst to me, she was with a small group of people who were going to jump into the pool fully dressed. This was the reason why she had decided to hold my hand. I never saw it coming; in a flash, I was in the pool with barely enough time to grab a breath. Now let's add insult to injury. Not only couldn't I swim, my belt at the time was a primary chain from a Harley Davidson Sportster, average weight roughly 30 pounds.

I landed exactly where you would think, right at the bottom of the pool. As I mentioned above, this experience was life-changing since it put me on a path to spiritual discovery. I was so shaken by it at the time that I rarely discussed it, perhaps only with a few relatives and close friends; however, my actions took a sharp turn that took me on a course of study I'm still involved with today.

If it wasn't for the watchful eye of my singer, Sandy, and the heroic effort of our friend Dimitri, I would be dead. I owe them both for my life.

I had nothing to leave anyone. At that point in my life, I was homeless, secretly living in rehearsal studios, recording studios, and boiler rooms in apartment buildings all through the West

Village of Manhattan. Shit, I even let my driver's license expire. It was a crazy time in my life for sure, of which misplaced pride and ego kept me from those I love and the life I wanted to live. That all changed once I stood up soaking wet at the edge of that pool.

So, what will it take to change you? Maybe this book will do the trick and open your eyes instead of waiting for some paradigm shift in your soul to take place. Sometimes, we all need a swift kick in the ass to put our heads on straight and take the blinders off. It is my sincere wish and hope that you take that first step and get some life insurance protection of those you leave behind. Please.

Chapter 13

Get Busy Living or Get Busy Dying

"Whoever plants a tree, winks at immortality."
- Felix Dennis

This will be the shortest chapter of this book because the title says it all. At the beginning of this book, I wrote of my brother's sudden passing and how it shocked me into taking action, to take stock of my own life and circumstances. This year will be especially tough because he won't be at our usual meeting place in Phoenix, where he lived, when I play the big round cement building in Glendale. There will be no lunch with him in catering, no big hugs when we'd say goodbye.

It is my most absolute sincerest wish that you take immediate action to protect yourself and your loved ones from what is inevitable. The big-money gigs are going to disappear, or will be harder to get and hold onto as you get older. You know it, and I know it. Time for one last bowl of Cheerios. So check this out,

I recently friended someone on Facebook who is in the position of placing musicians/sidemen into up-and-coming artists' bands. The average pay? About 400 bucks a week. The average age? Wait for it... 18 to 23. Do you think there's a box anywhere in this industry for any sideman from 23 to 28 to check off? Or maybe 28 to 35?

Not likely.

The reality is it's always been a young person's game, with a prerequisite on appearance, ability, and willingness to work for a low wage. Thank God that there are enough artists still out there who know the difference between merely playing or singing something and being able to sell it. To see real-life examples of this, check out Hired Gun-The Documentary. It's the real deal on how to live this kind of life, while picking up the check for it.

I hope you enjoyed this book as much as I did writing it. The inspiration for it was frightening yet exhilarating, with a pure sincere intention that you not wait for success in our industry before starting down the entrepreneurial highway to find another. Somewhere out there, someone is waiting for the answer you have, the solution to their problem. Bring it to them today, there's no need to wait any longer.

Ship
By J.F. Murphy

As I walk along the back streets of my life, I find myself upon my last sweet dying doorstep, I've led so many lives that my signature is faded. I've lost so many more that my graves are never empty. What my mind begins to fear you know my soul has got to know, to tear these doorsteps down, to dig these graves back up again. Are you waiting for your ship to come in, are you waiting for your life to begin?

Like the sun hunting through the leaves for a spot to rest, I'm like a naked stump praying for the fall to hide my nakedness, what my mind begins to fear you know my soul has got to know, to tear these doorsteps down to dig these graves back up again. Are you waiting for your ship to come in, are you waiting for your life to begin?

And so the circle turns until it's run its course and trots me out on some old leash to leave me with my thoughts, and if I sit and dry up, may God blow me away, for even in my dying there some living left to stay. What my mind begins to fear you know my soul has got to know, to tear these doorsteps down to dig these graves backup again. Are you waiting for your ship to come in? Are you waiting for your life to begin?

Epilogue
For Cathy

*"If you're going to walk on thin ice,
you might as well dance."*
- Karin Gillespie

These are some of the hardest and saddest words I've ever written. My dear, beautiful wife Cathy Eileen has passed. She slipped away in the early morning hours of May 12, 2015, next to me as we slept together that final night at home. She was my love, my companion, and my confidant for the last 17 years. Even as I write this, it doesn't seem real that she is actually gone forever.

She's left behind a legacy of smiles for everyone who knew her, her own and the many smiles she put on the faces of everyone who came in contact with her. In the end, even though her mind was sharp, her body was just too frail to continue. The ravages of multiple sclerosis had their way with her, but never took away her dignity and courage. She never allowed that to happen, she was a fighter and a scrapper all the way. That's one of the many things I loved about her.

Keep your guard up sweetie; true love forever and a day because you always put a smile on my face. Until then...

Ever Mine, Ever Thine, Ever Ours

Acknowledgements and Thanks…

God, Families and Friends. Of course, bandmates past and present, here and gone…If not for you all, my life would be empty. Thank you from the bottom of my heart forever. It will reflect. And most of all, my beautiful wife Cathy. My light, my love, my kick in the ass. I'll love you forever and a day.

Resources

Here are a few resources that have been helpful for me and my clients. If you did not get a chance to explore, watch, or purchase these resources while reading the book, here is a list of all of the resources mentioned within the chapters of *The High Paid Musician Myth*.

Websites:

- John O. Reilly Live - My website provides a clear strategy on how to survive your career with Success! http://www.johnoreillylive.com
- Amazon Kindle Direct Publishing - Independently publish with Kindle Direct Publishing to reach millions of readers. https://kdp.amazon.com/
- Fiverr - "What do you need done?" A great place to find basic help for your ebook needs. https://www.fiverr.com

Mentor Sites:

- Claude Diamond - Receive exclusive business advice from a great mentor. http://www.claudediamond.com/
- Eben Pagan - The Ultimate Guide to Eben Pagan's Products. Everything you need to know about business

growth, marketing, productivity and more. http://ebenpagan.info/
- Frank Kern - The Future of Internet Marketing. Breakthrough video and case study reveals exactly how to generate leads and turn them into customers at a profit. http://convertbook.frankkern.com/homepage/
- Gary Vaynerchuk - Gary builds businesses. He is also a prolific public speaker, delivering keynotes at events like SXSW. https://www.garyvaynerchuk.com/

Videos:

- *Hired Gun Film* - Fantastic documentary about a unique fraternity of musicians that possess uncommon musical ability, but who made a conscious decision to make a living playing music in relative obscurity. http://www.hiredgunthefilm.com/
- *Jeff Koons on Balloon Dog* - Interview with the artist about his work and inspiration. https://www.youtube.com/watch?v=dYahe1-isH4
- Damien Hirst on Charlie Rose - Interview with the artist about his spot paintings origins and exhibits. https://www.youtube.com/watch?v=o3DFRM1NgqQ

ABOUT THE AUTHOR

Photo credit Randy Brown

John O.Reilly is a lifelong professional musician/entrepreneur/rabble-rouser who, from early childhood, pushed the boundaries of his parents and legal conformity to its limits. Continually looking to create his own path by not accepting what is merely being presented to him as the truth, he's achieved what most musicians never do, success as a high paid hired gun in the music Industry.

With his company Maverick Musician LLC, John is in high demand for consulting, as well as speaking engagements. While not conforming to what "real world" society deems a successful person should look or act like, what he enjoys most is playing music, traveling, meeting new people, stimulating conversation, and performing business interventions.

To book John for consulting, or to speak at your next event, please call (570) 445-9161 or send an email to: contactoreilly@gmail.com

Learn more about John at http://www.johnoreillylive.com

Or, head to our Facebook page https://www.facebook.com/mavericklivemedia

If you would like to understand a little bit more about John, you can scan this nifty QR code below or text "maverick" to 58885.

Feel free to stay in the loop.

Printed in Great Britain
by Amazon